Stitched with Love

A Mother's Quilting Legacy

Stitched with Love

A Mother's Quilting Legacy

Robyn Pandolph

THE ELECTRIC QUILT COMPANY

Pandolph, Robyn
Stitched with love: a mother's quilting legacy / Robyn Pandolph
p.   cm.
ISBN 1-893824-06-3 (pbk.)

Published by The Electric Quilt Company
419 Gould Street, Suite 2
Bowling Green, OH 43402
www.electricquilt.com

Printed in China

Acknowledgments
Stitched with Love

Book

Executive Editor: Dean Neumann

Editor: Penny McMorris

Book and cover design: Jill Badenhop

Photography: Mark Packo

Photographic Assistant: Mark Kurczewski

Technical Editor: Margaret Okuley

Quilt construction: Robyn Pandolph, Margaret Okuley, Mary Lee Grabowski, Jane Murrell and Bonnie Wright

Quilting: Barbara Bradley and Cathy Nihiser

Layout Illustrator: Jared Oyer

Technical Proofreaders: Mary Beham, Karyn Hoyt, Lynn Koolish, Joyce Lytle, Peg Sawyer and Gretchen Schultz

Room stylings: Robyn Pandolph

Room settings graciously lent by:
Kirstin and Greg Sweeney, Bloomfield Hills, Michigan (Chapter 1 and *Abundant Earth*)
Eileen Bisbee, Findlay, Ohio (Chapter 2 and Chapter 4)
Diane Putnam, Glendale Flowers and Gifts, Toledo, Ohio (Chapter 3)
Mark Packo, Filmwerks Studios, Toledo, Ohio (*Abundant Earth* pillows)

CD-ROM

Software Development: Dean Neumann and Ann Rutter

Graphics: Neal Knueven

Quilt Variations: Margaret Okuley

Videographer: Tom Peru, Aztec Media Company, Colorado Springs, CO

Robyn would like to thank...

Bonnie Wright for sewing and assisting in various and numerous tasks.

My family: John, Zac, Eli, Joshua, and Hannah whose love and laughter inspire me continually.

Barbara and Gloria for their friendship and willingness to be included in the Twinkle Toes Trio.

Penny and Dean for all their support and encouragement.

Table of Contents
Stitched with Love

Chapter One
Treasures for Babies and Toddlers

Chapter Two
Childhood Holiday Memories

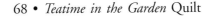

Chapter Three
Celebrating Growing Up

Chapter Four
New Beginnings

Photographer Mark Packo

Mark Packo, photographer, filmmaker and designer, began his career as an art director in New York City. He studied graphic design at Pratt Institute, Brooklyn, NY, and taught typographic design at Parsons School of Design, New York City. His still photography has been featured in numerous publications including *Metropolitan Home*, *Esquire* and *Communication Arts* magazines. His print, television and film work has won national awards, including an Emmy nomination for the PBS documentary, *Air Force One: The Planes & The Presidents*, which he produced and co-directed. His current photo and film production company, Filmwerks Studios, is located in a mid-nineteenth century former tobacco factory in Toledo, Ohio.

Biography
Robyn Pandolph

Robyn Pandolph is one of quilting's top designers. She's known for her popular fabric lines as well as her beautiful folk art appliqué patterns. Robyn loves old fabrics, primitive antiques, needleturn appliqué, and muted, vintage colors. She combines her loves in her company – Cabin Fever Designs. From her design studio in Colorado Springs, Colorado, Robyn creates appliqué patterns for quilts, pillows, wearables and accessories. The Cabin Fever Designs business office is in Friendswood, Texas, www.cabinfeverdesigns.com.

Her fabric has been extremely popular among quilters wanting a vintage look that works in any interior. Her lines, produced by Moda, include *Folk Art Wedding, Hannah's Garden, Summer Cottage, Rosehill Manor,* and *Folk Art Christmas.*

Robyn teaches needleturn appliqué in classes and workshops held around the country. She was a featured guest on the television program, *Simply Quilts* (HGTV – Episode 515) in the Fall of 1999.

Robyn lives in Colorado Springs, Colorado with her husband John, a software engineer, her three sons, Zac, Eli and Joshua, and her daughter, Hannah. The complete Pandolph family includes Hamlet the cat, and two great danes, Max and Maggie.

Introduction

Stitched with Love

I hope this book encourages you to use the creativity of handwork to tie together the generations of women in your family.

I am fortunate that my mother and grandmother passed down the tradition of handwork to me. I want to pass it on to my daughter, and hopefully one day, granddaughters. I want them to have joyful, self-expressive lives as they grow up in a world where rough edges can tear away at one's soul. I want to show you that you, too, have the ability to share the work of your hands with your daughters, granddaughters, nieces, and other women in your family, so that the tradition of handwork continues.

Hopefully our daughters will learn a better balance between personal contentment and the demands of others. Perhaps this is what we are experiencing now as women all over the world are making a determined effort to reacquaint themselves with the handwork that once was so vital to our survival.

No matter what a woman's profession, there is a place in her heart for handwork and the expression of individual creativity. It is a bond that links us to our past and will show future generations who we were.

I hope my designs convey this individualism and expression of love for those around me. I hope that these works of my hands will inspire and encourage you to take time to express yourself through the art of handwork.

Make time for the things that fulfill the creative woman in you.

Robyn

Robyn Pandolph

Practice Makes Perfect

"May the work of the hands delight the soul."

My passion is needleturn hand appliqué. Needleturn means that you use the needle to turn and tuck under the seam allowance of an appliqué patch as you stitch.

The more you do needleturn appliqué, the better you will get, and the smaller your stitches will be. Don't be concerned if your stitches show. I know a lot of appliquérs think you should hide the threads, and that nothing should be seen. But I really don't think that's important. I have quilts from the mid-1800s that show their stitches.

Historically, stitches showed a woman's needlework skills. Women were taught to sew so they could offer something of use to a man at the time of marriage. Women who weren't able to do good handwork weren't going to be a whole lot of help out on the farm or prairie. So small stitches showed your ability as a seamstress.

It's good for you, as a beginner, to understand that your stitches do show and they should show. Keep going, keep practicing, and your workmanship will get better and better. The more you do needleturn appliqué, the better you will get...

Appliqué Tips for Beginners

Beginners tend to be a little frightened of the black pen. Remember, the key to needleturn appliqué is in turning under the fabric. So if you're turning the black pen line under, there is really no reason to worry. As long as you don't see the line where it's turned under, you're fine.

Don't be afraid to trim your designs close to the fold line. Beginners often don't trim closely enough, leaving too much fabric. This causes wrinkles and bumps when the excess fabric is turned under, which keeps you from getting a smooth curve. Remember, you can leave more fabric if you want, at first, then trim as you stitch. As you learn and improve, you really need to trim closer to the line as you stitch, especially around small circles and outside curves. This will make it much easier for you to get smooth curves.

For inside curves, you don't have to worry quite as much about how much fabric is turned under. But you do need to clip rather closely. The tighter the curve, the more frequently you need to clip. Also, make sure you clip just through the black line. Remember to use your needle as a turning tool. Start on the far side of the curve, and just turn the whole curve under at once.

Needleturn Hand Appliqué Basics

Supplies

The supplies you will need for needleturn hand appliqué are simple and easy to find *(Figure 1)*.

- Pencil
- Freezer paper (available at any grocery store)
- Scissors for cutting paper
- Scissors for cutting fabric
- Scissors for trimming fabric - small scissors with sharp points that will help you get into the sharp points and the curves
- Ultra-fine point permanent markers
  Any color will do, I choose black for marking patches, and brown for writing on patches. You can use an acid-free pen, or any permanent marker from an office-supply store.
- Iron
- Glue
  Gluestick or Roxanne's Glue-Baste-It™
- Size 10 milliner or straw needle
- Thread
  I recommend silk thread if you can find it. Match the color to the appliqué patch, not the background fabric.
- Bias Press Bars®
  These are long strips of metal or nylon, in various widths, made for pressing bias tubes.

Figure 1

Figure 2

Printing the Pattern

The *Stitched with Love* CD, in the back of this book, contains the appliqué patterns for my projects. Print the patterns onto sheets of plain printer paper using your computer printer. If the pattern is too large to fit on one sheet of paper, the program will print as many sheets as needed. Dotted lines will show you where to overlap the pattern sheets. Match the dotted lines (cut off the overlap) to line up the pattern design. Tape the separate pages together, to form the overall pattern.

Tracing the Pattern

Put freezer paper, unwaxed side up, over your printed pattern design.

Trace each separate patch in your design onto a different section of freezer paper *(Figure 2)*, using a pencil. You'll want a separate freezer paper pattern for each patch in the appliqué design. Those patches that are stacked on the design will be separate on the freezer paper.

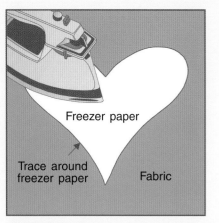

Figure 3

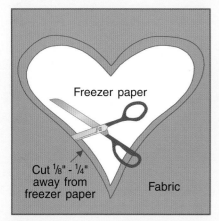

Figure 4

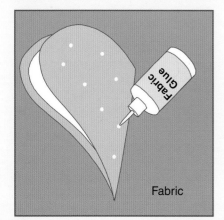

Figure 5

Cut the designs out of the freezer paper, cutting right along your tracing lines.

Spread out your fabric, right side up.

Put the freezer paper patterns onto the fabric, waxy (shiny) side down.

Put the iron on the wool setting and press the paper onto the fabric *(Figure 3)*. The wax helps adhere the paper to the fabric.

Trace a line around each paper design onto the right side of the fabric, using the permanent marker.

Multiple Designs

Appliquéing multiple designs, such as leaves or circles, is easier if you will number them on your pattern. Then, when you trace onto your freezer paper, use the same number on the freezer paper. That way you will know exactly where each piece goes.

Cutting

Cut out the design, cutting ⅛" to ¼" away from the marked line and freezer paper pattern *(Figure 4)*.

Glueing

Glue the wrong side of your fabric-freezer paper patches onto the right side of your background fabric, using a few dots of glue to hold the fabric in place *(Figure 5)*. Don't glue the edges down because you'll need to turn these under.

Peel off the freezer paper.

Apply the patches that go on top of one another, stacking them in the proper order.

Now you're ready to stitch.

Stitching

Thread a needle with thread the color of the patch to be appliquéd, and knot your thread end.

Turn under the edge of the appliqué patch with your needle, including the line that you've put on there *(Figure 6)*.

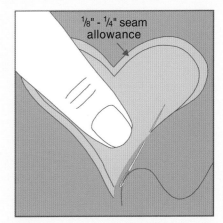

Figure 6

Start your first stitch by drawing the needle up from underneath the background fabric, bringing the needle right through the folded edge of the fabric that you turned under.

Stitch back down next to where you came up, but in the background not in the appliqué design *(Figure 7)*, making a small diagonal stitch, down and back up through the fold again.

Continue stitching in a counterclockwise direction, turning the raw edge under as you go.

The size of your stitch is not important when you first learn to appliqué. Your stitches will become smaller with practice. Be sure to use your needle as a tool for turning the raw edges of the appliqué patch fabric under.

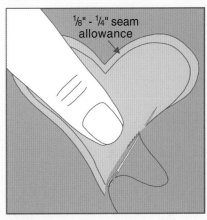

Figure 7

Corners

Inside curves – Clip inside curves right through the black marking line, at close intervals.

Outer curves – Trim away the seam allowance close to the black line, reducing the bulk of the fabric beneath the curve *(Figure 8)*.

Inner points – Clip through the seam allowance and black line, right to the point *(Figure 9)*.

Outer points – Trim away the seam allowance close to the black line.

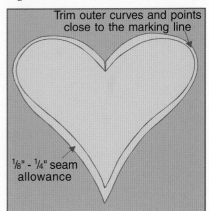
Figure 8

Tips:
If you find your fabric frays, don't trim it ahead of time. Wait until you get there with your stitching before you trim.

When appliquéing an inner point, make sure to take a stitch right where the clip is. Overcast the raw edge. You should only need to take one stitch. But, if you feel that you need more covering over the raw edge, take another stitch.

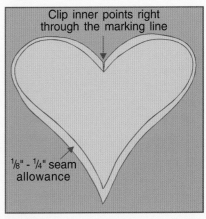

Figure 9

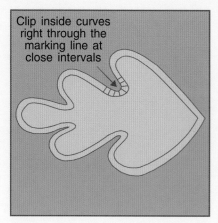

Figure 10

Inner Curves

The best thing to do is to clip at intervals through the lines. Make sure the clips are close together *(Figure 10)*.

When you appliqué, insert your needle on the far side of the curve, and with one sweeping motion, turn the whole curve. Then finger press with your thumb to hold the turned edge in place.

Appliquéing Circles

Before you begin, make sure to trim close to the line to eliminate the bulk beneath the circle, giving you smoother curves. Make sure to include the line when you turn. One key to getting smoother curves is taking stitches closer together. Remember, this is folk art appliqué, so you don't have to have perfect circles.

Star Points

Appliquéing star points or any other narrow point takes a little bit of practice.

As you are stitching, stop ⅛" from the end of the point. Take your last stitch in the background of the fabric leaving your needle free to stitch into your design. Turn your design, preparing to go the other direction on your point. This is where trimming is very important. Trim close to the black line to get rid of the excess fabric. Pull the point forward and trim away the seam allowance of the underneath fabric that you have already turned under. This will reduce the bulk of the fabric in the narrow point. Next, fold the point under, then turn under the other side, using your needle. Take a stitch at the very tip of your point, then take another stitch to secure the point in place.

Continue to stitch. If you find fraying threads sticking out, cut them with your scissors.

Practice makes perfect, so don't get discouraged.

Adding Dimension

Every little bit of dimension adds extra uniqueness to your quilt. Two ways of adding dimension as you appliqué are to use reverse appliqué, and to layer fabrics.

I especially like to use reverse appliqué on a piece that's rather large, like a leaf. It helps break up that space. You could just layer another piece on top. But it's just as easy to cut a hole and then turn under and reveal the background fabric.

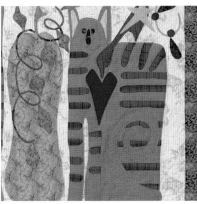

*On **Thanksgiving with Friends**, for example the cat's tail is layered on top of the cat's body, even though both are the same fabric print.*

Reverse Appliqué

Reverse appliqué is not as hard as it sounds. In reverse appliqué you cut a hole in the appliqué to expose the fabric beneath. When you trace the design onto freezer paper, be sure to also draw the opening onto the freezer paper (not as a separate piece), and cut out the opening. Lay the freezer paper onto the fabric and press. When you remove the freezer paper, slit the opening, leaving as much fabric as you can ($1/8$" to $1/4$" if you have it) *(Figure 11)*. Appliqué the hole just as you would the rest of the piece *(Figure 12)*.

You may want to use reverse appliqué to expose what's underneath. For example, you could do windows on a house in reverse appliqué, exposing a fabric layer beneath, to look like light coming through the window (as shown at left).

Layering Appliqué Patches

Layering pieces of the same fabric print also adds that little bit of dimension, adding to the quality of the appliqué design. The more complex your appliqué design, the more overlaying you will have. Remember you only need to appliqué the pieces where the edges are exposed. Edges that will be covered by another piece can be left raw. Appliqué the bottom layers first, then appliqué the top layers *(Figure 13)*.

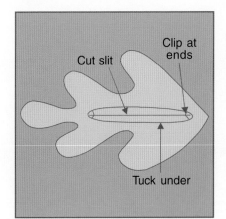

Figure 11

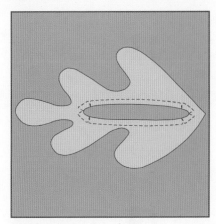

Figure 12

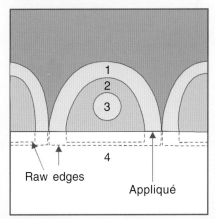

Figure 13

Vine Examples Using Bias Tubes

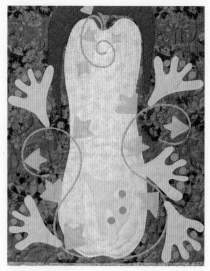

Fall Festival

Blessed Union

Guardian of Love

Bias Tubes

Bias tubes are long bias strips sewn into a tube. These tubes come in handy for appliquéing thin vines or stems and can be used in my projects wherever you need a thin curving line. (The vines in *Fall Festival*, page 48, *Blessed Union*, page 82, and the curly stems in *Guardian of Love*, page 92, are a few examples using $1/8$" bias tubes.)

To make a $1/8$" bias tube, cut a $3/4$" wide strip of fabric on the bias *(Figure 14)*. Fold it in half lengthwise, wrong sides together. Sew a scant $1/4$" seam parallel to the raw edges of the folded strip. Trim as close to the seam as possible. The seam will be hidden, so the more fabric removed the better *(Figure 15)*.

Once the seam is trimmed, insert a $1/8$" bias press bar into the tube. Roll the seam to the back of the bias bar, so it's hidden, and press with an iron. Use steam if necessary to make it flat. Slide the bias press bar through the tube as you press, always turning the seam to the back.

These bias tubes are easy to appliqué because they curve easily and the edges look finished since the seam is hidden.

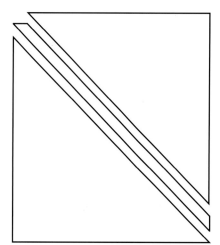

Figure 14
Cut $3/4$" strips on the bias.

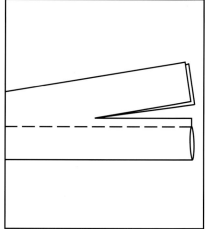

Figure 15
Fold wrong sides together. Sew $1/4$" seam; trim close to seam.

Binding

This is how I make binding to go around my quilts.

1. Add the combined measurement of all four sides of your quilt top.
2. Divide this number by 44" (the width of the fabric plus seam allowance).
3. If the number is uneven, round it up. For example, if you get 3.42, round it up to 4. This gives you the number of strips of fabric you need.
4. Cut a 2" strip for each width of fabric you need.
5. Sew these 2" strips end to end, right sides together, on the diagonal. Press flat.
6. Fold this 2" strip together lengthwise, wrong sides together. Press flat.
7. Sew the raw edge of the binding to the raw edge of the quilt, right sides together, taking a $\frac{1}{4}$" seam. Miter the corners as you stitch. Press the seam towards the binding.
8. Fold the binding over the seam so that the fold of the binding will be on the back of the quilt.
9. Slip stitch the binding in place along the seam line. Press.

Design Freely

What's exciting to me about appliqué is that it's so freeing. It's as if you can take a paintbrush and just paint on canvas. I do enjoy piecing, but it confines you to making edges and seams meet. It's more rigid, and has more rules.

You can have even more design freedom using the *Stitched with Love* CD that comes with this book. It lets you print the designs in any size you want, to use in all the ways I've suggested and more. Use the designs on floorcloths, curtains, pillows, slipcovers, tablecloths, cookies, gift tags and invitations as well as for quilts. Try them on clothes for fun. Make a jacket, and put a bee on your shoulder, or whatever you'd like. There are so many different ways to play with the images. I've even thought of stenciling the designs as borders around a room, rather than using wallpaper. Enjoy the freedom of appliqué, using my book and your computer.

Technical Support

The CD-ROM at the back of this book has been tested extensively. But custom computer configurations and software interactions vary so widely that unforeseen problems may be possible. Should you have any trouble installing or running the *Stitched with Love* CD-ROM, please contact The Electric Quilt Company for technical support:

Phone: (419) 352-1134 (Monday – Friday 9am – 5pm EST)
Fax: (419) 352-4332
E-mail: techsupport@electricquilt.com

Choosing Fabrics

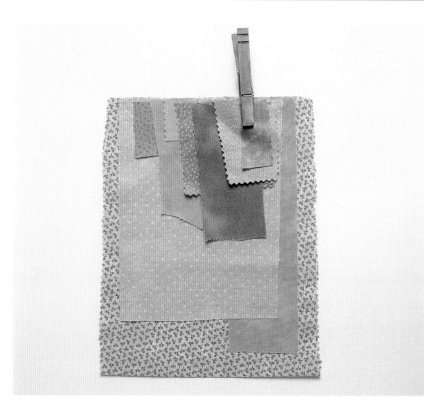

Since I design fabrics for Moda Fabrics, I like to use them in my quilts. But I also really enjoy the fabric of other designers. There's such variety, and I enjoy looking for different textures and colorations.

To make these other fabrics blend well with mine, I often bleach and overdye them. This dulls the colors, toning down bright colors and making white backgrounds look darkened by age – creating the vintage floral look I like, and making other fabrics work well with my own fabric lines.

A new twist on "baby colors" – pale gold, accented by moss green, pinks and blues for **Sweet Dreams***.*

Orange pumpkins provide a bright spark against more neutral creams, browns, olives and beet red in **Thanksgiving with Friends***.*

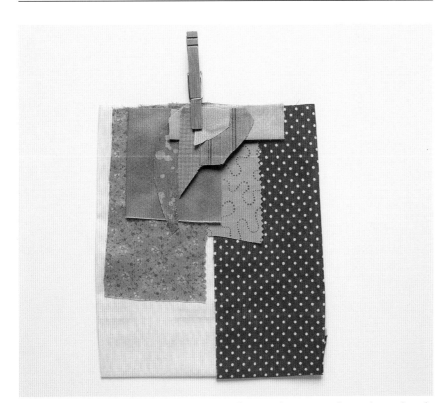

*The strong graphic look of **Teatime in the Garden** comes from dots, plus the sharp color contrast of red and white.*

The fabric I select for a quilt depends on what I'm making. I like to have a lot of variety of movement and texture in the quilt, and I enjoy challenging myself to get this. I don't mean high contrast prints, but subtle contrast. I like texture and some small motion in the background of the fabric. Without that, everything can appear to be flat. Make sure you use different types of prints so that each piece, like a leaf or a stem, stands out because of the movement in the print.

I don't like using brick fabric for a house or wood fabric for a roof or anything as specifically realistic as that. All quilts would look the same if you only used those realistic fabrics for specific parts of a design. I think it's more fun to just pick out odd pieces, and try them in different places, to see how they work.

*Sometimes a large floral suggests colors for the whole quilt, as it did for the softly colored **Blessed Union** wedding quilt.*

Bleaching for a Vintage Look

Before   *After*

Bleaching dulls bright prints, making colors look more like the soft, muted shades found in antique quilts.

To bleach, first test in the kitchen sink. Cut off a 2" square and test it. Use about a cup of bleach to 2 gallons of water. The longer the fabric stays in the bleach water, the lighter it will get (the opposite of dyeing Easter eggs), so keep checking the swatch to gauge how bleaching affects the fabric. You just want to downplay the brightness of the fabric, and make it look a bit old and worn.

Some people are concerned about what bleach does to the fabric. So if this concerns you, you may want to try a new product called Clorox® Advantage that has a guarantee that it will not break down the fiber of the fabric. You can also use one of the linen soaks made for taking the stains out of antique linens.

I normally do my bleaching in the washing machine. If I have a full load of fabric, I will use ½ cup of bleach. You can use ¼ cup if you don't have that much fabric.

If I find that the bleaching doesn't dull the colors enough, I may bleach one more time. But I won't do it more than twice, because I figure that it won't help and I don't want to destroy the integrity of the fabric.

Overdyeing for a Vintage Look

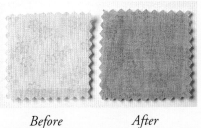

Before   *After*

Sometimes bleaching is enough to give you the look you want. But if you take the brightness away, and the fabric still doesn't really look aged, try overdyeing it with tan dye.

When I've finished bleaching a load of fabric and have it out of the washing machine, I see if some needs overdyeing. If so, I fill the machine with very hot water, and if it's a full load of fabric, I pour two boxes of tan Rit® dye (#16) in the water, let it agitate for a minute, then put my wet fabric in. I do all colored fabrics together, and it seems to work fine.

You can do a dye pretest in the kitchen sink by using ¼ cup liquid Rit® dye (tan #16) to a gallon of water.

Chapter One
Treasures for Babies and Toddlers

I was lucky enough to be born into a rich heritage of quilting, sewing, and handwork. Perhaps this is why I feel so passionate about sharing my love of quilting with you. My first memories of my grandmother are linked with her quilts and her quilting. The first thing we (my mom and I) did when we arrived at her house was go directly to her bedroom where she would open her armoire that was filled with quilts in different stages of assembly. My grandmother, mother and aunts all placed great importance on this needlework. I feel blessed to have learned early on the significance of expressing one's self through quilting.

As a mother of four, I feel honored to pass this down to my own children. This may not mean that they will choose to express themselves through quilting, but perhaps they will be aware of expressing their individuality through the creative work of their minds and hands. I made sure each of my children had their own special baby quilt when they were born. This is in remembrance of my first baby quilt that my grandmother made for me and that I still proudly own and display. My grandmother is no longer here physically, but the quilt she made for me is here to remind me of her love.

I hope that you, too, will feel a sense of deliberateness in creating a memory for your child, grandchild, or child of a friend. What a special way to carry your love through the years of a special loved one. Take time to start a legacy for your family.

Sweet Dreams

Finished Quilt Size: 38" x 50"

Fabric Requirements

- Appliqué block background squares & sashing – ½ yd. tan & white gingham
- Inner quilt border & binding – ⅔ yd. medium pink
- Outer quilt border – 1¼ yds. gold small floral
- Block borders – ½ yd. gold with white polka dots
- Small circles on block borders – fat quarter pale pink
- Triangles & large circles on block borders – ⅜ yd. pale green
- Backing – 1½ yds. pink & beige stripes

Scraps for Appliqué:

Moon Block
- Moon border – 6" sq. gold paisley
- Moon – 6" sq. pale yellow #1
- Star – 3" sq. pale yellow #2
- Circles – 4" sq. blue-gray

Bee Block
- Bee wings – 3" x 5" blue-gray
- Bee bodies – 3" x 4" pale yellow #1
- Bee stripes – 3" sq. medium gray

- Vine – 6" sq. dark green
- Leaves – 5" sq. green
- Outer flowers – 3" x 6" pink
- Inner flowers – 3" x 4" pale pink
- Flower centers – 3" sq. pale yellow polka dots
- Circle on vine – 2" sq. lavender

Butterfly Block
- Body – 2" x 5" medium gray
- Inner body – 2" x 4" gold paisley
- Upper wings – 5" x 7" light blue small floral
- Lower wings – 4" x 7" light yellow small floral
- Vines & leaves – 6" sq. green
- Circles – 5" sq. light blue
- Antennae – 4" sq. pale green
- Circles on antennae – 3" sq. blue-gray

Bird Block
- Bird – 6" sq. blue-gray
- Wing & tail feather – 5" sq. pale green
- Circles on bird – 3" sq. pale yellow polka dots
- Vine – 6" sq. tan print

- Leaves – 5" sq. green
- Berries – 4" sq. pale pink
- Circles on ends of vine – 3" sq. lavender

Flower Block
- Front petals – 6" sq. pale lavender print
- Back petals – 6" sq. lavender
- Circles on back petals – 4" sq. tan
- Outer flower center – 3" sq. blue-gray
- Inner flower center – 3" sq. gold paisley
- Circles on center – 4" sq. pale yellow #2
- Vine – 4" x 6" dark green
- Leaves – 4" sq. green
- Stem – 3" sq. dark green print

Star Block
- Star border – 6" sq. gold paisley
- Star – 6" sq. pale yellow #1
- Circles – 5" sq. blue-gray

Cutting Instructions

Block Background:
Cut six 6½" squares

Block Border:
Cut twelve 2½" x 6½" strips (top and bottom border)
Cut twelve 2½" x 10½" strips (sides)

Sashing:
Cut two 2½" x 22½" (horizontal sash)
Cut three 2½" x 10½" (vertical sash)

Inner Quilt Border:
Cut two 2½" x 22½" strips (top and bottom)
Cut two 2½" x 38½" strips (sides)

Outer Quilt Border:
Cut two 6½" x 26½" (top and bottom)
Cut three strips 6½" x 44"
Join them to make 2 side borders 6½" x 50½"

Quilt Binding:
Cut five 2" x 44/45" strips

Quilt Assembly Instructions

Sweater & hat by Ann Brogren of Right Off the Sheep, Birmingham, Michigan

Ann Brogren, who owns her own knitting and yarn shop, knit stars and crescents from the *Sweet Dreams* quilt into her original stocking cap and pullover set. Let the designs in my book, and on the *Stitched with Love* CD, inspire you in the same way.

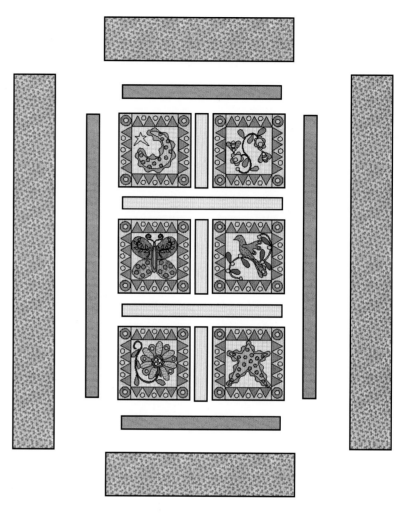

Block Assembly Instructions:

1. Appliqué center blocks, being careful not to extend your appliqué beyond the ¼" seam line.
2. Appliqué the triangles onto the outer block borders, matching inner raw edges.
3. Sew top and bottom block borders on each block. Press.
4. Sew side block borders on each block. Press.
5. Appliqué circles on block borders. (Circles are optional.)

Quilt Assembly Instructions:

1. Sew the vertical sashing strips between each pair of blocks.
2. Sew the horizontal sashing strips to the block rows.
3. Add the inner border top and bottom strips.
4. Add the inner border side strips.
5. Add the outer border top and bottom strips.
6. Add the outer border side strips to complete the quilt top.

Suggested Hand or Machine Quilting:
Outline blocks, borders and sashes. Meander quilting in outside border.

Sweet Dreams Floorcloth

Floorcloths are painted canvas "rugs." They were popular as floor coverings before linoleum was available, and they're coming back into style again.

If you want to make a floorcloth you must first buy a piece of canvas slightly larger than your finished floorcloth size, and enough gesso to cover the canvas. You can find canvas sold by the yard, and in different widths, in art supply stores. Gesso is an artist's medium that seals and stiffens the canvas. Gesso is just the general term for it. There are many different brands.

Take the canvas and gesso home, and build a simple wooden frame to hold the canvas. Pull the canvas tight over the front of the frame, bending it over the sides and stapling it to the backside of the frame. Then paint the gesso onto the canvas so that you have a surface that the paint won't soak into. The gesso stiffens the canvas and pulls it taut. That's why you need the frame – it really tightens up.

Print your design motifs from the *Stitched with Love* CD, then cut out and trace them onto your gessoed canvas. Paint on the design, and then put on 3 or 4 coats of clear polyurethane water-based finish over it. Matte is good if you don't want your rug to be glossy. When everything is dry, score along the edge of your design, take it off the frame, and turn the edges under. There are many different ways to finish the edges of your rug. You can sew a piece of fabric around the edge just like a quilt binding. Or you can do what I do, and glue the edge back, folding the corners so they're neat and trim.

You can put your rug on the floor and use it, and because of the polyurethane finish, you can clean it with soap and water just as you would clean a tile floor.

Fusible Web Appliqué

For quick appliqué projects, you can use fusible web. Fusible web is a paper-backed adhesive that bonds fabric together. It's available from most quilting and fabric stores. Fusing eliminates the need to turn under the edges of the appliqué piece, so you can quickly cut and fuse. It's perfect for clothing, pillows and blocks to frame.

When fusing, it is important to follow the manufacturer's directions. There are various brands of fusible web, and the iron heat setting and pressing times may vary.

1. Trace the design onto the paper side of the fusible web. Because the fusible web will be ironed to the back side of the piece, the pattern must be reversed when tracing. You may trace from the backside of the master pattern using a lightbox to accomplish this. A lightbox is a translucent surface over a light source, like a lamp under a glass tabletop, or a sunny window. Each element of the design must be traced separately onto the fusible web. It is helpful to group pieces that will share the same fabric close together. You may wish to number the pieces to aid in placing the similar shapes later.

2. Roughly cut the traced shapes apart, leaving a margin beyond the traced line. Follow the manufacturer's directions to fuse the pieces to the wrong side of your chosen fabric. The iron touches the paper side of the fusible web. The rough side goes against the fabric.

(Continued on page 31)

Sweet Dreams Backpack

*Fuse my designs to decorate anything you make. I made this **Sweet Dreams** backpack (perfect for a diaper bag) using a purchased pattern designed by my friend Leslie Gladman. Her company, Favorite Things, calls this backpack pattern "A Faithful Companion" (#032). The pattern makes a roomy, lined backpack with adjustable button straps, a zippered pocket in the flap and 2 inside pockets.*

I used oatmeal-colored linen for the backpack, and a pink polka dot fabric for the lining. Before I completed the bag I fused on designs from the *Sweet Dreams* quilt – using a 6" butterfly on the bag's flap, and 3" flowers and 1½" bees on the bag. To finish it off, I used a pink ribbon drawstring, and a variety of buttons to close the bag and pockets.

You can order the backpack pattern (#032) from:

Favorite Things
6455 60ᵗʰ Avenue
Delta BC
Canada V4K 4E2

Favorite Things
145 Tyee Drive
Suite 184
Port Roberts, WA 98281-9602

http://favoritethings.net

Or check with your favorite quilt shop!

Wearable Art

*Printing motifs from the **Stitched with Love** CD and fusing the fabric designs onto purchased clothing turns plain clothes into wearable art.*

This little hat and overall set is decorated with the same bees and blossoms used on the floorcloth.

(Continued from page 30)

3. Cut out the shapes fused on the fabric along the traced line. Use sharp scissors to make clean cuts. A small scissors is helpful for the small pieces and the thin vines.

4. To arrange the appliqué, lay the background fabric on top of the pattern layout. If necessary, use a lightbox to see the lines clearly. Arrange the appliqué pieces in place on the background. Using the pattern paper as a tray, move the project to the ironing board, so the design will not be disturbed. Fuse the pieces in position with the iron.

5. The edges of the fused pieces may be stitched in place with a narrow zigzag stitch using matching thread. You may also use a decorative machine stitch like the buttonhole stitch in black or a contrasting color. Use a tear-away stabilizer under the project when stitching. If the project will not be laundered, it may not be necessary to secure the edges.

Stars & Crescents Curtains

Figure fabric and ribbon yardage:

1. Measure window width. Multiply by 2 or 3, depending on the curtain fullness you want.

2. Divide your step #1 answer by 48" – the approximate width of voile.

3. Round any uneven number up to the next full number. For example, round 2.19 up to 3. This is the number of lengths needed.

4. To figure length, measure the length of your window plus 6".

5. Multiply your step #4 answer by the number from step #3. This gives you the number of inches of fabric you need to buy.

6. Divide the width you got in step #1, above, by 5. Multiply this by 18. This gives you the number of inches of ribbon you need to buy.

Cutting and sewing instructions:

1. Cut a 5" strip of fabric down the whole length of the fabric. Set aside for the facing.

2. Cut the rest of the fabric into lengths equal to your step #4 measurement.

3. Seam these pieces together, making the width of your curtain. Press seams open.

4. Fuse dots, stars and crescents to the curtain.

5. Seam the 5" long strip to the top of your curtain to make a facing. Cut off excess. Press flat to the back.

6. Hem curtain sides 1".

7. Cut the bottom of the curtain in large points. The pictured curtains have 2 points per section.

8. Fuse stars along the top of the curtains, spaced 5" apart.

9. Cut two parallel 1" horizontal slits in the center of each star, 1" apart, all the way through star, curtain and facing.

10. Thread ribbons through both slits, starting from the back, and tie firmly around the curtain rod.

*Print the stars and crescent moons (suggested size: 6") and the simple star for the curtain top (suggested size: 3.5") from the **Stitched with Love** CD.*

These beautiful, filmy curtains require very little sewing and no bottom hemming. They're made of off-white polyester voile, a decorator fabric usually sold on a tube in fabric stores, perfect for bed canopies as well.

Sweet Dreams Blocks

I framed four 10" blocks from the *Sweet Dreams* quilt to show you another way you can use my block designs. If you are planning to frame blocks, you don't have to finish the edges. You can just fuse the appliqué design, if you'd like, and if you want it to look like it's stitched, just use a pen and do that.

Once you've made the block, cut a piece of foam-core board as large as your quilt block. (Get the adhesive kind of foam-core where you peel the paper off – available in craft and art supply stores.) Cut a piece of batting slightly larger than your block. Put it onto the board, pulling it taut. Pull the excess around to the back. Put your quilt block on top, and pop it into a frame. These blocks work great for decorating.

The frames I show here were made from old fence boards from Texas. I love their look. When we lived in Texas, we had a fence that needed replacing, and a friend came and collected all my fence boards. He took them home, and now makes frames out of all those weathered boards. You can find pre-made weathered frames in different hobby and craft stores. And you can paint them, as I have. I put a color that is brighter and more dominant underneath. Then I put another color on top of that. Next, I sanded it so that I could see the brighter color coming through. Finally, I put an antiquing gel or wax finish on top. The colors I used for the *Sweet Dreams* frames were buttermilk yellow over dark green.

Bee Block

Butterfly Block

Bird Block

Have a room without a view? Try hanging a framed block in the window rather than on the wall. You'll block the view while still letting in light.

To hang the framed block, attach two metal screw-in eye hooks along the frame's top edge. Thread ribbon through each eye. Attach the ribbon to the window frame from small nails or decorative tacks.

Flower Block

Chapter Two
Childhood Holiday Memories

My mom was very good at creating holiday memories. She was not a quilter. I think maybe she thought she could not measure up to the skills of her mother, but my mother could do many things that made our holidays stand out among my memories.

Every Christmas my mother would decorate (in great detail) the sugar cookies she baked for our school Christmas parties. She was always my room mother, so she always appointed herself to bring the cookies. I remember a Santa cookie with a bag of toys. My mom would detail his clothing and toys in the bag with icing. I've tried to duplicate this feat and have found a renewed admiration for my mother's talent and the time she was willing to spend, when in the end her work was eaten up by unimpressed first graders.

At least a quilt is around year after year to remind everyone that you consider your family worthy enough of your time and talents to create a tradition for them during the holidays.

I hope that you will be inspired by the designs in this book to not only make a quilt that everyone will remember when they visit for the holidays, but that you will also take time to let your children, nieces, nephews, and grandchildren participate in the process of creating the quilt. If the children are too young, then maybe making sugar cookies and decorating them together would be better. Then they can always watch you quilt while they enjoy munching on their creations.

Abundant Earth (Easter)

Finished Quilt Size: 36" x 36"

Fabric Requirements

- Inner quilt border – ½ yd. blue & off-white gingham
- Outer quilt border – ¾ yd. tan & blue small floral
- Backing – 1¼ yd. yellow and off-white gingham
- Binding – ⅓ yd. medium blue
- Rabbit block background – fat quarter gold floral

Scraps for Appliqué:

Rabbit Block
- Rabbit – 12" x 16" beige & tan stripes
- Circles on rabbit – 6" sq. medium blue print
- Eye – 2" sq. cranberry
- Inner ear – 3" x 8" pale pink print
- Star – 5" sq. tan print
- Stems – 12" sq. gray plaid
- Flowers – 6" sq. lavender stripe
- Centers – 4" sq. pale yellow polka dots
- Leaves – 6" sq. pale green

Carrot Block
- Block background – 6½" x 12½" gold paisley
- Carrots – 6" x 10" orange print
- Carrot tops – 8" sq. green print
- Heart – 3" x 5" light pink
- Flower – 3" sq. lavender stripe
- Center – 2" sq. pale yellow polka dots
- Stem – 3" sq. gray plaid
- Leaves – 3" sq. pale green

Bee Skep Block
- Block background – 8½" x 12½" gold print
- Bee skep – 8" x 12" pastel stripes
- Stripes on skep – 8" x 12" pale yellow
- Door – 4" sq. blue-gray
- Star – 4" sq. beige & tan stripes
- Stems – 4" x 12" gray plaid
- Leaves – 6" sq. pale green
- Flowers – 6" sq. lavender stripe
- Centers – 4" sq. pale yellow polka dots

Bee Blocks
- Block background – 12" sq. small blue & off-white gingham
- Setting triangles – 12" sq. tan & blue small floral
- Head – 2" sq. blue-gray
- Bee body – 6" sq. pale yellow
- Bee wings – 6" sq. tan
- Stripes – 4" sq. gray plaid
- Stinger – 3" sq. brown

Bird Block
- Block background – 12½" x 12½" light gold
- Bird & wing – 12" sq. blue-gray
- Circles on bird – 3" sq. tan print
- Branch & stems – 12" sq. brown windowpane check
- Leaves – 8" sq. dark green
- Flowers – 8" sq. dark pink print
- Inner flowers – 6" sq. pale pink print
- Flower centers – 4" sq. gold

Cutting Instructions

Rabbit Block Background:
Cut one 12½" x 18½" block

Carrot Block Background:
Cut one 6½" x 12½" block

Bee Skep Block Background:
Cut one 8½" x 12½" block

Bee Blocks Background:
Cut three 4½" blocks (background)
Cut twelve 2½" squares (setting triangles)

Bird Block Background:
Cut one 12½" x 12½" block

Inner Quilt Border:
Cut two 2½" x 24½"
(top and bottom)
Cut two 2½" x 28½" (sides)

Outer Quilt Border:
Cut two 4½" x 28½"
(top and bottom)
Cut two 4½" x 36½" (sides)

Quilt Binding:
Cut four 2" x 44/45" strips

Bee Block Assembly

1. Mark a diagonal sewing line across the wrong side of all four setting triangle squares.

2. Place a small (setting triangle) square on a corner of the large (background) square – right sides together – so that the diagonal sewing line is lined up as shown *(Figure 1)*. Line up the raw edges on top and side.

3. Stitch along the marked sewing line. Trim the seam, fold the corner back to make a triangle, and press the block flat.

4. Do the other corners as shown *(Figures 2 – 5)*.

5. Appliqué a bee in the center of each block.

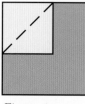
Figure 1

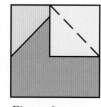
Figure 2

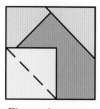
Figure 3

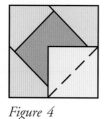
Figure 4

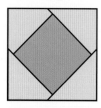
Figure 5

Quilt Assembly Instructions

Block Assembly Instructions:
1. Sew three Bee blocks.
2. Appliqué the bee to the pieced Bee blocks.
3. Appliqué the other blocks to their backgrounds.

Quilt Assembly Instructions:
1. Sew the Bee blocks together, as shown.
2. Sew the Rabbit block to the Carrot block.
3. Sew the Bee Skep block to the Bee block row, then add the Bird block.
4. Add the inner border top and bottom strips.
5. Add the inner border side strips.
6. Add the outer border top and bottom strips.
7. Add the outer border side strips to complete the quilt top.

Suggested Hand or Machine Quilting:
Echo quilting in and around appliqué designs. Outline quilting along inner border. Meander quilting in outside border.

Kids love making holiday things in the kitchen. Even little ones, too young to be anything but underfoot, can become helpers by threading gift tags onto strings to tie around gift jars of purchased or homemade honey, jam, sauces or candies.

Add some fun to ordinary sweatshirts with my appliqué designs. See another decorated sweatshirt on page 77. As you read through this book, I hope you'll see that my designs can be used on a wide variety of projects — sewn, knit, painted, or printed.

Use the *Stitched with Love* CD to print out gift tags and labels following these easy steps.

1. Print out a colored block picture to use for your label or tag. The pictured labels were printed 2" square; the tags were printed 2¾" square.
2. Paste the label onto the jar, using rubber cement. Tip: You can print onto large self-stick Avery® label paper, to make self-sticking labels and tags.
3. Paste the tag onto a sheet of stiff paper. (Manila folders make good tag backings.) Using an X-Acto® knife, or sharp scissors, cut the tag out so that no background paper shows along the tag edge.
4. Punch a hole at the top-left corner of the tag.
5. Thread cord or ribbon through the hole.
6. Write "To:" and "From:" on the tag's back side.

To make "jar bandanna" toppers:
1. With a pinking shears, or regular scissors, cut out a square of fabric for the topper. The pictured jar used a 6" fabric square.
2. Center the fabric square on the jar lid and fasten over the lid with a rubber band around the jar neck.
3. Tie the ribbon or cord (with tag) over the rubber band, looping it several times around, if necessary, to hide the rubber band.

Natural Egg Dyeing

Your children or grandchildren can have fun dyeing eggs the old-fashioned way – with natural fruit and vegetable dyes. These make-them-yourself dyes give eggs soft "vintage" colors that look beautiful in old stoneware or wooden bowls.

1. Hard-boil eggs, and cool.
2. Put a cup (for light colors) or more (for dark colors) of one of the following fruits or vegetables into a saucepan.
   - Spinach - green
   - Yellow onion skins - yellow
   - Blueberries - blue
   - Beets – pink
3. Add water to cover an inch or more.
4. Bring water and fruit or vegetable to a boil.
5. Reduce the heat and simmer for 15 minutes to an hour, until the color is as dark as you would like.
6. Strain the colored water into a bowl.
7. Add about a tablespoon of vinegar for each cup of liquid.
8. Dip the hard-boiled eggs into the dye. The longer they stay in the dye, the darker they will become.
9. Remove the eggs when they are the color you want, and let them dry.
10. Refrigerate eggs until egg-hiding time.

Abundant Earth Pillows

Carrot Pillow

Fabric Requirements:
- See page 39 for block background and appliqué fabric requirements
- Pillow back and linings – ½ yd. gold & off-white check
- Inner pillow cover – fat quarter tan
- See page 45 for border fabric requirements

Cutting Instructions:
- Carrot pillow linings – Cut three 8½" x 14½" gold & off-white check
- Carrot inner pillow – Cut two 6½" x 12½" tan

Finished Pillow Size: 8" x 14"

Bee & Buds Pillow

Fabric Requirements:
- Block background – fat quarter tan & blue print
- Pillow back and linings – ⅝ yd. gold & off-white check
- Inner pillow cover – ⅝ yd. tan
- See page 45 for border fabric requirements

Scraps for Appliqué:
- Star – 4" sq. gold & off-white check
- Stems – 4" x 12" dark green
- Leaves – 6" sq. pale green
- Flowers – 6" sq. light blue & off white check
- Bee body – 2" sq. pale yellow print
- Bee stripes – 2" sq. dark gray
- Bee wings – 3" sq. tan
- Bee stinger – 1" sq. brown
- Bee head – 1" sq. blue-gray

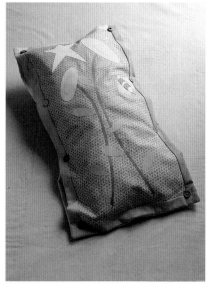

Finished Pillow Size: 11" x 20"

Cutting Instructions:
- Bee & Buds block background – Cut 9½" x 18½"
- Bee & Buds pillow linings – Cut three 11½" x 20½" gold & off-white check
- Bee & Buds inner pillow – Cut two 9½" x 18½" tan

Abundant Earth Pillows

Finished Pillow Size: 10" x 14"

These little "button-on" pillow slipcases are fun to make. The inner pillow, front, and back are all made separately, stacked like sandwich layers, and held together by buttons.

Bee Skep Pillow

Fabric Requirements:
- See page 39 for block background and appliqué fabric requirements
- Pillow back and linings – ½ yd. gold & off-white check
- Inner pillow cover – fat quarter tan
- See page 45 for border fabric requirements

Cutting Instructions:
- Bee Skep pillow linings – Cut three 10½" x 14½" gold & off-white check
- Bee Skep inner pillow – Cut two 8½" x 12½" tan

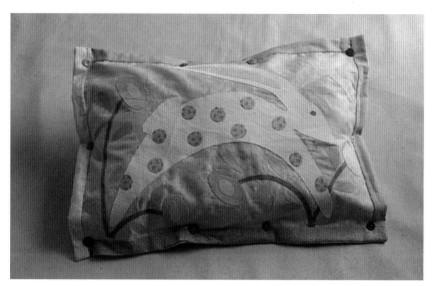

Finished Pillow Size: 20" x 14"

Rabbit Pillow

Fabric Requirements:
- See page 39 for block background and appliqué fabric requirements
- Pillow back and linings – ⅝ yd. gold & off-white check
- Inner pillow cover – ⅝ yd. tan
- See page 45 for border fabric requirements

Cutting Instructions:
- Rabbit pillow linings – Cut three 14½" x 20½" gold & off-white check
- Rabbit inner pillow – Cut two 12½" x 18½" tan

Bird Pillow

Fabric Requirements:
- See page 39 for block background and appliqué fabric requirements
- Pillow back and linings – ½ yd. gold & off-white check
- Inner pillow cover – ½ yd. tan
- See page 45 for border fabric requirements

Cutting Instructions:
- Bird pillow linings – Cut three 14½" x 14½" gold & off-white check
- Bird inner pillow – Cut two 12½" x 12½" tan

Finished Pillow Size: 14" x 14"

Border Assembly Instructions

Top border

Right border

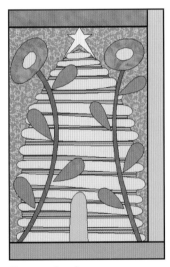

Bottom border

Left border

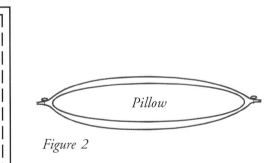

Figure 1

Pillow

Figure 2

Fabric Requirements for Borders:
- ⅛ yd. dusty pink
- ⅛ yd. light pink print
- ⅛ yd. pale green
- ⅛ yd. gray blue print
- 8 buttons for large pillows; 6 buttons for small – ½" to ⅝" buttons in different colors
- Loose polyester batting

Cutting Instructions for Borders:
- Cut 1½" strips of each of the 4 colors

Assembly Instructions:

1. Appliqué one of the blocks from the *Abundant Earth* quilt.

2. Sew borders to the block. Sew one border strip to the top side of a block, right sides together. Trim ends. Sew the second border strip to the block's right side; the third border strip to the bottom; the last border strip to the left side. Trim each border to fit, and press flat, before adding the next.

3. Sew the bordered block to one of the pillow lining rectangles, right sides together, leaving a 4" opening for turning *(Figure 1)*. Turn right sides out. Sew the opening closed. Press flat.

4. Sew two pillow lining rectangles together, turn and press as in step #3.

5. Sew inner pillow rectangles together, as in step #3. Stuff with loose polyester filling to make a pillow before sewing opening closed.

6. Sandwich the stuffed pillow between the pillow front and pillow back. Sew buttons at the corners and evenly spaced on the sides, going only through the pillow cover front and back, but not the pillow itself *(Figure 2)*.

Fall Festival (Halloween)

Finished Quilt Size: 20" x 40"

Fabric Requirements

- Appliqué block background & binding – 1 yd. green floral print
- Quilt border & backing – 1 yd. tan & green print
- Cat – fat quarter dark gray stripe
- Large pumpkin – fat quarter pale orange print

Scraps for Appliqué:
- Moon – 5" sq. tan print
- Bird – 8" sq. blue & tan gingham
- Star – 4" sq. gold paisley

- Bird legs & star hanger – 3" sq. brown print
- Small pumpkin – 7" sq. pale orange plaid
- Leaves – 14" sq. pale green
- Vines - 16" sq. or ⅛" bias tubes light brown print
- Pumpkin stems – 4" sq. brown
- Pumpkin blossoms – 15" sq. gold dot print
- Pumpkin blossom circles – 8" sq. gold & green plaid

Cutting Instructions

Block Background:
Cut one 16½" x 36½" block

Quilt Border:
First cut: cut three 2½" strips 44" wide
Second cut: cut two of the strips 40½" long
Cut one strip to make two 16½" long strips

Quilt Binding:
Cut three 2" x 44/45" strips

Quilt Assembly Instructions

Even the smallest holiday celebrants can have fun working on their own "quilt" – a coloring book page printout which matches the holiday wallhanging you're making. Using the *Stitched with Love* CD, print out a stack of these uncolored outline drawings, put out the crayons, and let them color while you quilt.

This sample page was colored by Lindsey Nelson, daughter of Jan Nelson, The Electric Quilt Company's Shipping Manager.

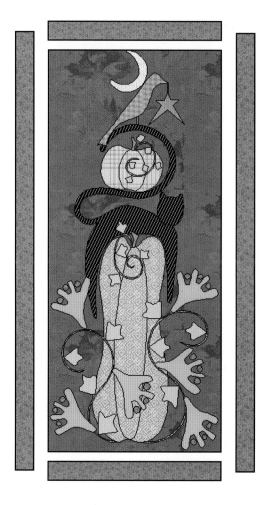

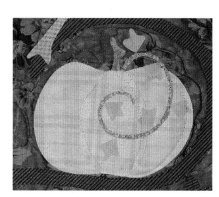

Block Assembly Instructions:
The ovals in the center of each pumpkin are the same color as the pumpkin. This layering is intended to add dimension, making the pumpkin look fuller.

Quilt Assembly Instructions:
1. Sew the top and bottom border to the center block.
2. Add the side borders to complete the quilt top.

Suggested Hand or Machine Quilting:
Echo quilting in and around appliqué designs. Meander quilting in block background. Serpentine quilting in border.

Parchment Luminarias

These uncolored printouts make handsome candle coverings. For "stained glass" luminarias, let kids color the parchment printouts with crayons.

Add a warm glow to any room in your home by turning paper printouts, votive candles, and everyday drinking glasses into holiday luminarias.

Using the *Stitched with Love* CD, print my motifs as outline drawings – printed "landscape" so the length of the paper wraps around the glass. Print onto transparent parchment paper or vellum, using your computer printer. (A laser printer is required for vellum.) Use the pumpkin and cat designs from *Thanksgiving with Friends* for a Thanksgiving table centerpiece (shown). Or dress your winter holiday mantle with *Winter's Sentry* snowmen and stars. Parchment and vellum papers are available at most art supply, craft or rubber stamp stores.

Wrap the paper printout around a drinking glass. This works best if the glass has straight vertical sides, rather than sloped. Fasten the paper with transparent tape where it overlaps in back.

Place a votive candle into the glass. Light the candle. Since you'll need to reach the match all the way down into the bottom of the glass, use long fireplace matches if you have them. Or use tweezers to hold the lit match to reach the candlewick.

The shadowy colors in Fall Festival take on a warm glow when seen by candlelight.

Finished Quilt Size: 36½" x 32½"

Fabric Requirements

- Appliqué block background & outer quilt border – 1¼ yd. off-white floral print
- Inner quilt border – ⅓ yd. dark green & gold seaweed print
- Large pumpkin – fat quarter pale orange print
- Backing & binding – 1⅓ yd. dark green with gold polka dots
- Pumpkins – fat quarter orange print
- Vine (pumpkins) – fat quarter medium green print #1
- Vines (birds) – fat quarter pale green
- Birds – fat quarter dark green plaid
- Cat stripes – fat quarter brown plaid
- Cat bodies, tails & feet – ⅓ yd. brown & blue gingham

Scraps for Appliqué:
- Cat eyes & nose – 6" sq. dark brown paisley
- Cat inner ears – 6" sq. tan print
- Hearts on cats – 6" sq. dark red
- Leaves (pumpkins) – 12" sq. medium green print #2
- Stems (pumpkins) – 5" sq. gold paisley
- Stars – 8" sq. pale yellow
- Leaves (birds) – 12" sq. dark green
- Berries (birds) – 8" sq. cranberry

Cutting Instructions

Block Background:
Cut one 20½" x 24½" block

Inner Border:
First cut: cut three 2½" x 44" strips
Second cut: cut two 2½" x 20½" (sides) from one strip
Cut two 2½" x 28½" (top and bottom) from the other two strips

Outer Border:
First cut: cut four 4¾" x 44" strips
Second cut: cut two 4¾" x 28½" (top and bottom) from two strips
Cut two 4¾" x 32½" (sides) from the other two strips

Quilt Binding:
Cut four 2" x 44/45" strips

Quilt Assembly Instructions

I want the quilting to flow, so that's why I choose cotton batting. I know there used to be a misconception about batting, that the more loft the better, but that's really not what I want. I want thin batting. So I use very thin 100 per cent cotton batting that has been needlepunched.

I don't use any batting that hasn't been bleached out or that has any of the flecks of the natural cotton. To me, it seems harder to quilt.

Another batting you might want to try is one that blends cotton and wool. The lanolin that's naturally in the wool helps your needle glide. Either all cotton or wool and cotton are good battings to use.

Quilt Assembly Instructions:
1. Sew side inner borders onto the quilt. Press. Trim.
2. Sew top and bottom inner borders onto the quilt. Press. Trim.
3. Sew top and bottom outer borders onto the quilt. Press. Trim.
4. Sew side outer borders onto the quilt. Press. Trim.
5. Appliqué the design onto the border.

Suggested Hand or Machine Quilting:
Echo quilting in and around appliqué designs. Meander quilting throughout the rest of the quilt.

Winter's Sentry (Christmas)

Finished Quilt Size: 28" x 32"

Fabric Requirements

- Border stars and snowman body – $^{7}/_{8}$ yd. tan floral
- Border stars and block background – 1 yd. light blue with off-white polka dots
- Backing – 1 yd. blue & tan stripes
- Binding – $^{1}/_{3}$ yd. pink small floral

Scraps for Appliqué:

Snowman
- Cheek – 3" sq. pale pink #1
- Eye – 2" sq. dark green #1
- Nose – 2" x 4" pale pink #2
- Arm & twig – 3" x 12" light brown print

Snowman's Clothes
- Hat – fat quarter pale pink print
- Hat trim – 3" x 9" tan print
- Circles on hat – 8" sq. light blue & pink plaid
- Pom-pom – 4" sq. tan print

- Shoulder piece – 7" sq. tan print
- Vest armhole piece – 6" sq. pale pink print
- Belt – 7" sq. light blue & pink plaid
- Hearts on belt – 7" sq. pink small floral
- Vines on clothes – 12" sq. dark green #1
- Leaves on clothes – 8" sq. pale green

Tree and Vines
- Tree branch & twigs – $^{1}/_{8}$ yd. light brown print
- Star vine – fat quarter medium brown print
- Stars – 12" sq. pale yellow
- Leaves on star vine – 8" sq. dark green #2
- Leaves on twig – 6" sq. dark green #3

Cutting Instructions

Block Background:
Cut one $20^{1}/_{2}$" x $24^{1}/_{2}$" block (blue with off-white polka dots)

Pieced Star Block Border:
Piece 26 blocks
Finished block measures $4^{1}/_{2}$"

Center squares: cut 26 – $2^{1}/_{2}$" squares (tan floral)
Star points: cut 208 – $1^{1}/_{2}$" squares (tan floral)

Background squares: cut 104 – $1^{1}/_{2}$" squares (blue with off-white polka dots)
Background points: cut 104 – $1^{1}/_{2}$" x $2^{1}/_{2}$" rectangles (blue with off-white polka dots)

Quilt Binding:
Cut three 2" x 44/45" strips

Star Point Assembly

Pieced Star Border

There are 26 star blocks in the border of *Winter's Sentry*. For each star block you will need to do the following:

Star Point Assembly Instructions:

1. Mark a diagonal sewing line across the wrong side of all of the star point (tan floral) squares.

2. Place a star point square on the top-left corner of a background point rectangle (blue with dots) – right sides together – so that the edges match and the diagonal sewing line is lined up as shown *(Figure 1)*.

3. Stitch along the marked sewing line.

4. Trim ¼" away from the seam *(Figure 2)*.

5. Fold the corner back to make a triangle, and press the seams toward the squares *(Figure 3)*.

6. Place another star point square on the top-right corner of the same rectangle – right sides together – so that the edges match and the diagonal sewing line is lined up as shown *(Figure 4)*.

7. Stitch along the marked sewing line.

8. Trim ¼" away from the seam *(Figure 5)*.

9. Fold the corner back to make a completed star point, and press the seams toward the squares *(Figure 6)*.

10. Once you have all the star points assembled, follow the steps below to make the star blocks.

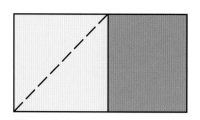

Figure 1

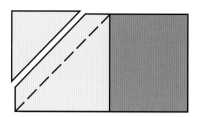

Figure 2

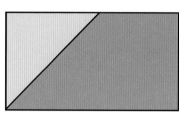

Figure 3

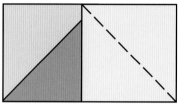

Figure 4

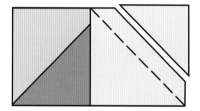

Figure 5

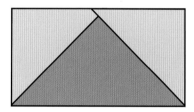

Figure 6

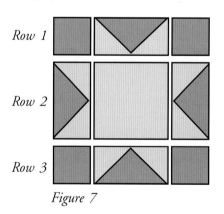

Figure 7

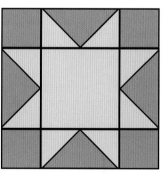

Figure 8

Star Block Assembly Instructions:

1. Line up 4 star points, 4 background squares, and a center square on the table in 3 rows, as shown *(Figure 7)*.

2. Row 1: Sew one 1½" background square (blue) to each end of a star point, right sides together. Press seams toward the background squares.

3. Row 2: Sew one star point to each side of the center square, right sides together. Press seams toward the center square.

4. Row 3: Sew one 1½" background square (blue) to each end of a star point, right sides together. Press seams toward the background squares.

5. Sew Row 1 to Row 2, right sides together. Press seams toward Row 1.

6. Sew Row 3 to the bottom of the block to complete the block. Press seams toward Row 3 *(Figure 8)*.

Quilt Assembly Instructions

Clearly fun! Let kids decorate with homemade holiday window cling decals. All you need is the *Stitched with Love* CD, an ink jet printer, and ready-to-print clear decal sheets. Try Hammermill Papers'® Invent it!™ clear decal sheets, available in many art, office supply, and even grocery stores.

The pictured snowman and stars were printed in the original colors from the *Winter's Sentry* quilt. Kids could have fun coloring holiday motifs themselves, printing, then arranging their artwork on a window for all to see.

These cling decals stick to any dry, smooth surface – windows, mirrors, file cabinets, even the refrigerator. They won't leave sticky stuff behind, are easy to move, and can be stored and reused.

To print clings, set the printer to Transfer, Glossy, Photo or Transparency mode, and print on the clear side of the decal sheet. Let dry completely before peeling away the backing paper.

Quilt Assembly Instructions:
1. Sew 26 pieced star blocks for the star border.
2. Sew 5 blocks together to make the top border. Sew the top border to the quilt center.
3. Sew 5 blocks together to make the bottom border. Sew the bottom border to the quilt center.
4. Sew 8 blocks together to make the right border. Sew the right border to the quilt center.
5. Sew 8 blocks together to make the left border. Sew the left border to the quilt center to complete the quilt top.

Suggested Hand or Machine Quilting:
Outline all appliqué and pieced patches.

Victorian Salt Clay Icicles

The whole family can have fun making these ornaments, made by rolling salt clay between your hands to form long thin icicle shapes.

*These pale ribbons coordinate with the **Winter's Sentry** wall quilt. For a more Victorian look you could use dark velvet ribbons.*

2 cups salt
²/₃ cups water
1 cup cornstarch
¹/₂ cup cold water
Paper clips or ornament hooks

1. Mix the 2 cups salt and ²/₃ cup water together in a saucepan. Stir constantly over low heat for about 4 minutes (do not boil). Remove from heat.

2. Quickly mix 1 cup cornstarch and ¹/₂ cup cold water together in a bowl, and add this combination to the heated mixture, stirring quickly. If the resulting mixture is not a thick paste, place it back on low heat and stir for about a minute until the mixture is dough-like.

3. Knead the salt clay dough on a flat surface until it is as smooth and pliable as bread dough. If you don't want to form it immediately, store the dough in plastic or foil and keep it in an airtight container.

4. Form the icicles by rolling small bits of dough between your hands to make long, thin and pointed icicle shapes. Stick a paper clip or ornament hook into the icicle top while the dough is still soft.

5. Let the icicles dry for 2 days at room temperature. Or, to dry quickly, preheat the oven to 350° F, turn the oven off and place the icicles in the oven on a wire rack. Leave them inside until the oven has cooled off.

Victorian Salt Clay can also be rolled out like cookie dough and cut with a cookie cutter.

Recipe used courtesy
http://www.makestuff.com

Chapter Three
Celebrating Growing Up

It seems that our "advanced" societies do not set aside a certain time in the lives of our adolescent children to signify their step into adulthood. This to me is a tragic oversight on our part. Somewhere between the time our children learn to walk, and the time they walk down the aisle, we expect them to change from child to adult with no special act or celebration. It is my wish that we make an effort to celebrate this crossover in responsibility and expectation. There are many ways to do this, some of which my husband and I have tried. My oldest three children are boys. My husband and I decided that when each one turned 13 he would take them on a two week backpacking trip into the Pecos Mountains of New Mexico. It was not always easy, but they knew that this was our way of acknowledging their changing into men. My daughter, on the other hand, decided that to acknowledge her turning into a woman at 13, she and I would take a shopping trip to New York.

There are other ways to celebrate these times, such as tea parties for girls so that learning social graces becomes something they enjoy and accomplish before they are put on the spot. I think it would be a great idea for a grandmother to host a tea party for her grandchildren and in doing so include some stitching activities for them to learn. This, too, is something that we as a society have decided is unimportant and yet many young girls turn into women wishing they had been taught how to quilt or sew. Take time to share your gifts with others.

Finished Quilt Size: 42½" x 42½"

Fabric Requirements

- Appliqué block background – ³/₄ yd. off-white
- Contrast block background – ³/₄ yd. tan & red floral print
- Quilt border, binding, teacups, corner circles – 1½ yd. red with off-white polka dots
- Backing – 1¼ yd. red & tan stripes
- Flower stems – fat quarter dark green #1

Scraps for Appliqué:
- Circles on cup – 8" sq. off-white
- Tea in cup – 6" sq. dark green #2
- Large hearts – 14" sq. pink small floral print

- Small hearts – 10" sq. pale green
- Bee wings – 6" sq. brown & blue gingham
- Bee bodies – 6" sq. yellow
- Bee stripes – 4" sq. blue-gray
- Leaves – 12" sq. dark green #2
- Flowers – 10" sq. medium blue stripes
- Inner flowers – 8" sq. light blue stripes
- Flower centers – 6" sq. pale yellow
- Tea bag string – 4" sq. medium brown

Cutting Instructions

Appliqué Block Background:
Cut four 12½" squares

Contrast Block:
Cut one 12½" square for the center block

Side Setting Triangles:
These are the triangles in the center of each side of the quilt. These triangles should be quarter-square triangles so straight grain is on the longest side.

First cut: cut one 18¼" square
Second cut: cut square diagonally in both directions so that you will have 4 triangles

Corner Setting Triangles:
These are the 4 triangles on each corner of the quilt.

First cut: cut two 9³/₈" squares
Second cut: cut each of these in half diagonally

Quilt Border:
First cut: cut four 4½" x 44" strips
Second cut: cut two 4½" x 34½" (top and bottom) from two strips
Cut two 4½" x 42½" (sides) from the other two strips

Quilt Binding:
Cut four 2" x 44/45" strips

Quilt Assembly Instructions

Antique appliqué quilts were often quilted with an overall design. But I prefer my quilts to emphasize the appliqué, so I normally quilt just around the edge of the designs, then quilt the backgrounds more heavily to make the appliqué stand out.

Sometimes you will have to quilt through several layers of fabric. Since I sometimes layer fabrics and don't cut out the fabric from behind the design, you could have layers upon layers. But normally the smaller pieces are on the very top, so you won't have a whole lot of quilting to do on them.

Row 1: A, B, & C
Row 2: D, E, & F
Row 3: G, H, & I

Quilt Assembly Instructions:
1. Sew row 1 as shown.
2. Sew row 2 as shown.
3. Sew row 3 as shown.
4. Sew the three rows together.
5. Sew the corner setting triangles to the four corners.
6. Add the top and bottom border.
7. Add the side borders to complete the quilt top.

Suggested Hand or Machine Quilting:
Echo quilting in and around appliqué designs. Meander quilting throughout the rest of the quilt.

Bud Vase Chair Slipcovers

I enjoy appliquéing circles, and using them in my designs, because the continual line of the circle keeps the design moving. Perhaps it has more to do with the gentle whimsy of circles. They create a fun look in my designs and yet are simple in form.

Then again, maybe it is more complex than that since circles represent our own lives and the cycle we experience as time goes by.

You can create a casual slipcover by appliquéing the polka dot bud vase design (suggested size: 14") onto a 2½ yard length of fabric, and draping it over a chair. For a pattern for a more shaped slipcover, contact Cabin Fever Designs, phone: (281) 992-8118, http://www.cabinfeverdesigns.com.

Teatime Tablecloth

Fabric Requirements:
- Background – 1¼ yd. off-white
- Border – ¾ yd. red polka dot

Cutting Instructions:
- Cut 44" square for center of cloth
- Cut five 4½" strips for border.
  Piece to make:
  Two 4½" x 44"
  Two 4½" x 52"

Assembly Instructions:
Appliqué the heart and bee motif onto each corner of the tablecloth center square. These can be fused or done by hand. The words "Tea Time" are written with ink on the heart. Use red ink for the look of redwork embroidery.

Stitch the top and bottom borders to the center square of the tablecloth. Stitch the side borders on next. Hem the border edges by turning them under ¼" twice and stitching.

The tablecloth is used over a 30" round table that is covered with a floor length cloth.

The Teatime tablecloth is a 44" square of fabric with 4" borders. The corner appliqué is a variation of the heart from the quilt, with an enlarged bee in the center (suggested motif size: 10").

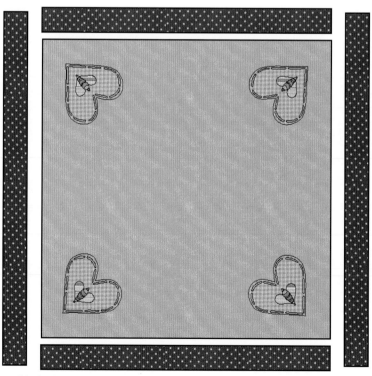

Tablecloth Assembly Diagram

Teatime Invitation Instructions

Supplies for each invitation:
- Laser printer (necessary for printing on vellum – inkjet printers will not print on vellum)
- One 8½" x 11" sheet of paper printed with a colored design (choose a pale color, so it won't make the words of your invitation hard to read)
- Two 8½" x 11" sheets of vellum (a stiff, translucent paper)
- Clear vellum envelope (not shown)
- 8" of satin ribbon

Preprinted papers, vellum and vellum envelopes can be purchased at most art supply, craft or rubber stamp stores. Depending on your invitation size, you may be able to get two invitations from an 8½" x 11" sheet of paper.

Instructions for making invitations:
1. Open your word processing program on your computer, type out whatever words you want on your invitation, using a hard return to make each printed line begin and end it where you would like.
2. Print a test copy of your invitation words onto a plain sheet of regular paper. See how the font, size, and style look. With a ruler, measure the length of the longest line of type. If the line is too long to properly fit the invitation size you have planned, reformat or resize the typed lines.
3. Print your properly sized words onto a sheet of vellum, using a laser printer.
4. In *Stitched with Love*, select the motif you want to print, sizing it to fit across your printed words. (Kirstin used the heart and vine from the *Blessed Union* quilt (see Chapter 4).
5. Print a test copy of your motif onto a plain sheet of regular paper. See how the design looks beneath the invitation words.
6. Print your properly sized motif onto a sheet of vellum, using a laser printer.
7. Using an X-Acto® knife, or old rotary cutter you can use to cut paper, and a plastic or metal ruler, cut out your three papers:
   - Bottom layer: colored paper back sheet
   - Middle layer: design on vellum
   - Top layer: words on vellum

Cut the bottom layer sheet ½" wider and taller than the middle and top layers. Kirstin's bottom layer was 6" W x 7½" H. Her middle and top layers were 5½" W x 7" H.
8. Stack the layers, carefully positioning them so an edge of the bottom layer shows on all sides, then punch two holes for the ribbon, positioning the holes as shown in the picture.
9. Thread ribbon through the holes, tying on top in a square knot, or in a bow. Kirstin tied her ribbon with the reverse – dull, not shiny – side out, to give the ribbon a more antique look.

Invitations by Kirstin Neumann Sweeney, Bloomfield Hills, Michigan

Designer Kirstin Neumann Sweeney used the *Stitched with Love* CD and her word processing program to make filmy, ribbon-tied party invitations. Pick out your favorite motifs from the CD. Use them for everything from birthday parties to anniversary celebrations, holiday cards, or even wedding invitations. By choosing special ribbons and background papers, you'll create invitations lovely enough to become keepsakes.

Teatime Cookies and Favors

This is my mom's cookie recipe:
12 dozen cookies

8 cups flour
5 teaspoons baking powder
1 teaspoon salt
3 cups sugar
4 teaspoons vanilla
4 eggs & milk to make $1\frac{1}{3}$ cups
$1\frac{1}{3}$ cups oil

1. Sift flour, baking powder, and salt into a large bowl.

2. Blend the oil into the dry ingredients with a pastry blender or a fork.

3. In a separate bowl, mix sugar, vanilla, eggs, and milk. Beat together until light and fluffy.

4. Stir into flour/oil mixture. Chill about one hour or so.

5. Roll out on floured surface to about $\frac{1}{4}$" thick and cut as desired. Bake 9 minutes at 400° F. Decorate.

This recipe can be halved for fewer cookies, but remember that if you are using a large cookie cutter you will need plenty of dough.

Helpful hint: before chilling, press dough into a large flat circle. Wrap with plastic wrap and chill. This will make it easier to roll out without cracking.

*Print the cookie pattern from the **Stitched with Love** CD, paste it onto cardboard, cut out around the design, and use as a shape for cookie cutting. Suggested size for this big cookie: 6".*

*Create party favors by placing cookies in clear glassine bags, tied with a ribbon and card. Kirstin Neumann Sweeney printed the heart and vine motif on these cards from the **Stitched with Love** CD. See page 73 for her matching party invitations.*

Teatime Sandwich Loaf by Lucretia Vandemark, North Baltimore, Ohio
It's easy to turn everyday sandwich ingredients into a fancy party sandwich loaf.
The hardest part may be finding a tray or platter to hold your creation.

Polka Dot Teatime Cake by Kirstin Neumann Sweeney, Bloomfield Hills, Michigan

Bread:

Any loaf of unsliced bread will do. Lu used old-fashioned white and honey wheat, for color contrast.

Cut the crust from all sides of the bread so that you have a "brick of bread."

Slice the bread horizontally. Before you slice the bread, you need to decide how many layers you want to have and how thick you want them to be. You don't want the finished loaf to be much more than 5" high, or it will be difficult to cut and may not fit on a luncheon plate.

Fillings:

It's up to you. Any spreadable filling will work.

Some suggestions: egg salad, ham salad, cheese and pimento, chicken salad, tuna salad, grated vegetables with yogurt.

Assembly:

Butter bread on both sides before spreading fillings if your loaf must stand for awhile. This keeps the bread from getting soggy. Stack up the layers: bread, filling, bread, filling, bread... Be sure to spread the filling an even thickness all the way out to the corners.

Frosting:

Whip an 8 ounce package of cream cheese with a little milk. Start with 2 tablespoons of milk, adding more, until the cream cheese is a good consistency for spreading. Lu added some food coloring for a salmon color.

Frost the sandwich loaf - just like icing a cake. Garnish with parsley, olive slices, carrot curls, pepper rings, etc.

Teatime Sweatshirt

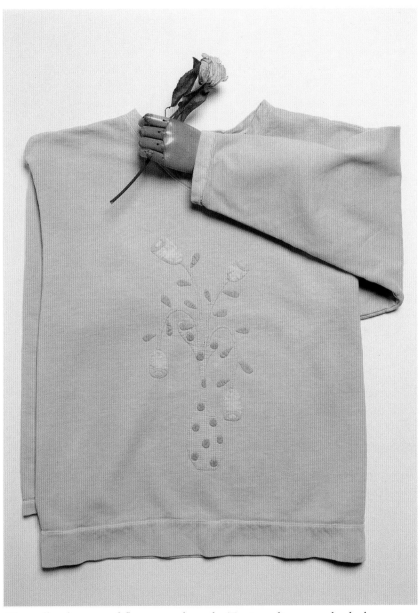

Painted pot by Molly Allen
Birmingham, Michigan

Gardener/photographer Molly Allen freely painted motifs from the *Stitched with Love* CD to give clay pots and saucers a colorful folk art look. Molly painted with acrylic paint inside the saucer, down to the rim, letting the clay show below. She painted the pots outside, and about an inch inside, down to the "dirt" line.

The polka dot vase of flowers used on the Teatime slipcovers also looks great on a sweatshirt. See another appliquéd sweatshirt on page 41.

Chapter Four
New Beginnings

Weddings! My day is coming I know. So far, though, it is a distant thought, but one that I should start working on right now. I want to make each of my children a wedding quilt. What a wonderful way to reaffirm my love for them and the special one they choose to spend the rest of their life with.

My mother and I spent many happy hours picking out the fabric and assembling my wedding dress. We each sewed on it in the days before my wedding. There were many things shared in those hours of sewing that proved to be quite beneficial to me as a young wife. Not only did I learn a lot from my mother during that time, but I sensed a confidence in myself and her that no matter what the future held, our relationship would remain strong.

Join together with a son or daughter who is preparing to take this huge step in their lives, to create a wedding quilt. The time you share together will be beneficial to each of you.

Maybe just a gift of your love through a quilted wall hanging or small quilt will be all they need, to know that you are there for them.

Blessed Union

Finished Quilt Size: 66" x 85"
(Twin Size)

Fabric Requirements

- Block background & sashing – 4 yds. off-white
- Quilt border – 1½ yds. pink floral print
- Backing – 5 yds. tan & pink floral print
- Binding – ½ yd. dark green

Appliqué:
- Hearts – ½ yd. pink small floral print
- Vines – ¾ yd. dark green (vines are made with ⅛" bias tubes)

- Leaves – ½ yd. green plaid
- Flowers – ½ yd. pale pink print
- Flower centers – fat quarter pale pink
- Inner flower – fat quarter pale yellow
- Ribbon – fat quarter pale green
- Bird – ¼ yd. medium blue
- Wing – ¼ yd. blue & off-white gingham

Cutting Instructions

Sashing:
(Cut from length of fabric before cutting blocks)
Vertical sashing: cut two 73½" x 3½" strips
Horizontal sashing: cut nine 16½" x 3½" strips

Block Background:
Cut twelve 16½" squares

Quilt Border:
Cut seven 6½" strips the width of the fabric
Piece to make top and bottom
Two 6½" x 54½"
Two 6½" x 85½"

Quilt Binding:
Cut seven 2" x 44/45" strips

Collecting Primitive Antiques

I have always appreciated primitive American antiques for their history and character. In fact, one of the reasons I started my own quilt pattern company was so I could have extra spending money for antiques. These were the things that people made themselves, usually, because the stores were too far away or there just wasn't enough money for nice furniture. I feel a kindred spirit with these people from times past. Their sweat and blood was what kept them going year after year, and to think that I can have a part of that in my home is very humbling.

Since I am from Texas originally, most of the antiques that I have collected were purchased in Texas. Many of them I found at Round Top, Texas, which is an absolutely fantastic antique fair. Fields and fields of antiques and junk can be picked through over the first weekend in October and the first weekend in April throughout an area in Central Texas. The occasional rainstorms and the ever present Texas heat makes the adventure even more memorable.

If you are ever near Round Top, Warrenton, Shelby, Carmine, etc. on either of these weekends make sure you take time to get out in the fields to find a treasure.

Quilt Assembly Instructions

Block Assembly Instructions:
Appliqué 12 blocks. Write a different wish on each heart's banner after the blocks are appliquéd, but before the quilt is quilted. For instructions on doing this, see the *Blessed Union* Inscriptions instructions on page 85.

Quilt Assembly Instructions:
1. Sew the blocks together in vertical rows, inserting a short sashing strip between each block. You choose which word goes next to another.
2. Sew the block rows together, inserting a long sash between each row.
3. Add the top and bottom border.
4. Add the side borders to complete the quilt top.

Suggested Hand or Machine Quilting:
Outline the appliqué and sashes. Quilt borders in design of your own choice.

Blessed Union Inscriptions

Peace   *Laughter*

Honor   *Harmony*

Understanding   *Love*

Honesty   *Unity*

Joy   *Humility*

Health   *Abundance*

The *Blessed Union* quilt carries twelve wishes for the wedding couple's happy life together. Each block holds a different wish, written or embroidered on the tiny banner that wraps around the heart.

The wishes are written out on this page for you to trace. Notice that the longer words, such as "Understanding," "Abundance," and "Laughter," are slightly arched in the middle, making them fit the curved banner.

1. Trace the words from this book onto paper, using a dark pen.
2. Place the paper on a light table, a glass tabletop with light shining from below, or tape to a windowpane, right side up.
3. Place one of the cutout banner patches onto one of the words, positioning it to center the words onto the banner.
4. Trace the words onto the fabric banners using a pencil.
5. Appliqué the banners onto the heart blocks.
6. Embroider or trace over the words with a brown Pigma pen. Test the pen's colorfastness by writing onto a scrap of fabric. Iron the scrap to heat set the ink, then wash the scrap. See that the ink does not run or fade.
7. Lay the finished heart block on a square of fine sandpaper or sandpaper board to keep the fabric from moving while you write. Use the brown Pigma pen to write on each banner, following the pencil lines you've traced for each word.
8. Iron the banner to set the ink.

Blessed Union Pillow

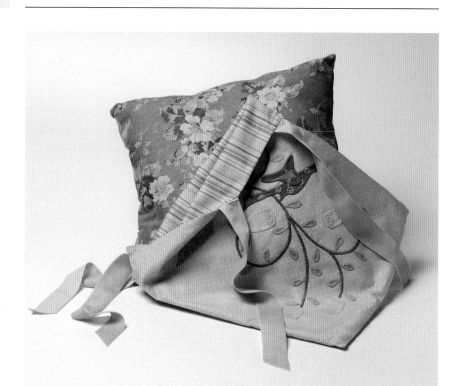

This lined pillowcase covers a finished pillow. The pillowcase ties loosely onto the pillow with ribbon ties, letting the pillow and lining peek through the side opening. Choose three fabrics – one for the pillow, a second for the pillowcase lining, a third for the appliquéd pillowcase cover. It's the combination of these fabric prints, and the ribbon texture, that makes this a wonderful accent pillow.

Fabric Requirements:
- Pillowcase outside – ½ yd. gold with off-white polka dots
- Pillowcase lining – ½ yd. pink & tan stripes
- Inner pillow cover – ½ yd. green floral
- Ribbon ties – 2½ yds. of 1¾" wide pink velvet ribbon
- 1 package loose polyester stuffing

Scraps for Appliqué:
- Heart – 5" sq. pink small floral
- Flowers – 5" sq. pale pink small floral
- Inner flowers – 3" sq. pale pink
- Flower centers – 3" sq. yellow with dots
- Vine – 12" sq. dark green
- Leaves – 10" sq. pale green
- Bird & wing – 8" sq. olive stripe
- Circles on bird – 6" sq. blue-gray
- Star – 3" sq. gold paisley

Cutting Instructions:
- Pillowcase outside – Cut two 16" x 14" rectangles
- Pillowcase lining – Cut two 16" x 14" rectangles
- Inner pillow cover – Cut two 15½" x 13½" rectangles
- Ribbon ties – Cut six equal lengths

Finished Pillow Size: 16" x 14"

Pillow Assembly Instructions

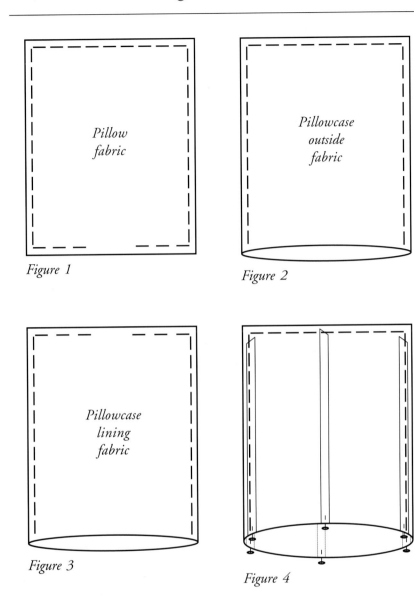

Figure 1

Pillow fabric

Pillowcase outside fabric

Figure 2

Pillowcase lining fabric

Figure 3

Figure 4

Figure 5

Assembly Instructions:
Appliqué the bird, vine and heart design to one pillowcase outside rectangle.

Pillow:
Sew the two inner pillow cover rectangles to each other, right sides together, leaving a 5" opening along one of the short sides *(Figure 1)*. Turn right side out. Insert pillow stuffing to make a pillow as firm as you'd like. Hand-sew the opening closed.

Pillowcase Outside:
Place the pillowcase outside rectangles right sides together, and sew along three sides, leaving one short side open *(Figure 2)*.

Pillowcase Lining:
Place the pillowcase lining rectangles right sides together, and sew as shown *(Figure 3)*, leaving an opening 4" long in the center-bottom seam for turning. Turn the lining right side out.

Pin ribbon pairs near both side seams and at center, around the top edge of right side of lining, matching raw edges of ribbon end and lining *(Figure 4)*. Insert the lining (with ribbons) into the pillowcase, right sides together. Stitch all around the top edge, catching the ribbon between lining and outside *(Figure 5)*. Turn the pillowcase right side out through the bottom opening. Hand-stitch the opening closed. Insert the stuffed and covered pillow into the pillowcase. Tie ribbons to close.

A Day to Remember

Finished Quilt Size: 30" x 42"

Fabric Requirements

- Appliqué block background – ¾ yd. tan floral
- Quilt backing & binding – 1⅔ yd. pink small floral print
- Quilt border – ½ yd. green with pink flowers

Scraps for Appliqué:
- House & chimneys – 13" sq. pale pink brick print
- Roof, door & windows – 10" sq. blue-gray print
- Window panes & door panels – 6" sq. pale yellow
- Heart on house – 5" sq. light pink
- Vines on house – 15" sq. dark green #1
- Leaves on house – 8" sq. green plaid
- Smoke – 6" sq. pale blue
- Moon – 8" sq. gold paisley
- Bird – 7" sq. gray plaid
- Star – 3" sq. gold print
- Name & date – 6" x 14" tan
- Large scallops – 10" sq. green plaid
- Small scallops – 8" sq. pink
- Circles on scallops – 6" sq. blue-gray print
- Sunflower petals – 8" x 12" blue & gold gingham
- Sunflower centers – 5" x 10" gold
- Sunflower dots – 8" sq. blue-gray
- Stems – 3" x 20" dark green #2
- Leaves – 10" sq. dark green #1
- Hearts on quilt – 8" x 12" pale pink print
- Circle flowers in box – 6" sq. lavender
- Flower centers – 4" sq. gold plaid
- Leaves – 6" sq. pale green

Cutting Instructions

Block Background:
Cut 24½" x 36½"

Quilt Border:
First cut: cut four 3½" strips 44" wide
Second cut: cut two of the strips 24½" long (top and bottom)
Cut two of the strips 42½" long (sides)

Quilt Binding:
Cut four 2" x 44/45" strips

Painted Breakfast Tray

Painted tray by Ann Kelly
Bloomfield Hills, Michigan

Painter Ann Kelly reinterpreted the designs on *A Day to Remember*, painting a wooden tray perfect for a bride and groom's honeymoon breakfast.

Quilt Assembly Instructions:
1. Sew the top and bottom border to the center block.
2. Sew the side borders to complete the quilt top.

Suggested Hand or Machine Quilting:
Outline quilting around appliqué; meander quilting in block background. Continuous heart design around border.

Write your own inscriptions on the quilt. I suggest using a brown Pigma marker to write the bride's name on one heart, the groom's name on the other heart, and the wedding date on the center banner. My quilt banner reads: "Joined in Marriage on this the 27th day of January in the Year of our Lord 1979. Peace be to this Union."

Fabric Finches

These fabric finches make great Christmas tree decorations, or they can perch inside during the winter on bare tree branches you bring inside and "plant" in a large sand-filled planter. Spray the branches lightly with white paint if you'd like.

Fabric Requirements:
- Scraps of fabric (about 8" x 14" for each bird)
- 2 tiny beads for eyes
- Polyester stuffing

Fold the fabric in half, crosswise, right sides together. Draw the bird onto fabric. DO NOT CUT. Machine or hand stitch along the line, leaving an opening between the marks. Cut the bird out about 1/4" away from the line you've sewn. Clip the curve at the neck. Turn right side out. Sew the oval base to one side of the opening with the narrow end towards the tail. Stuff the bird with batting. Sew the remaining side of the oval base, closing the opening. Sew beads on for eyes.

To hang the bird, sew a ribbon at the middle of the back. To "perch" the bird, as shown, thread a thin wire through the bird's base.

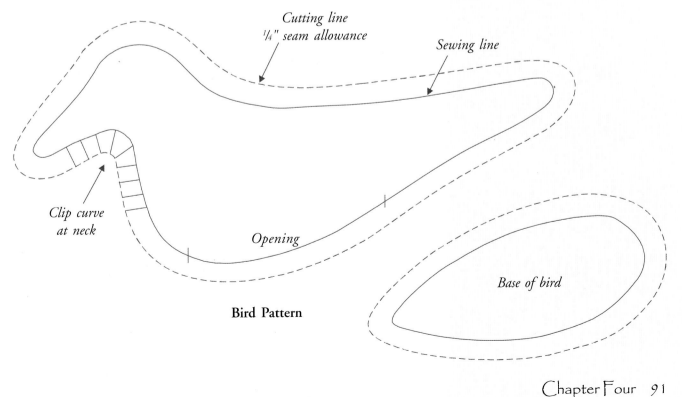

Cutting line
1/4" seam allowance

Sewing line

Clip curve at neck

Opening

Bird Pattern

Base of bird

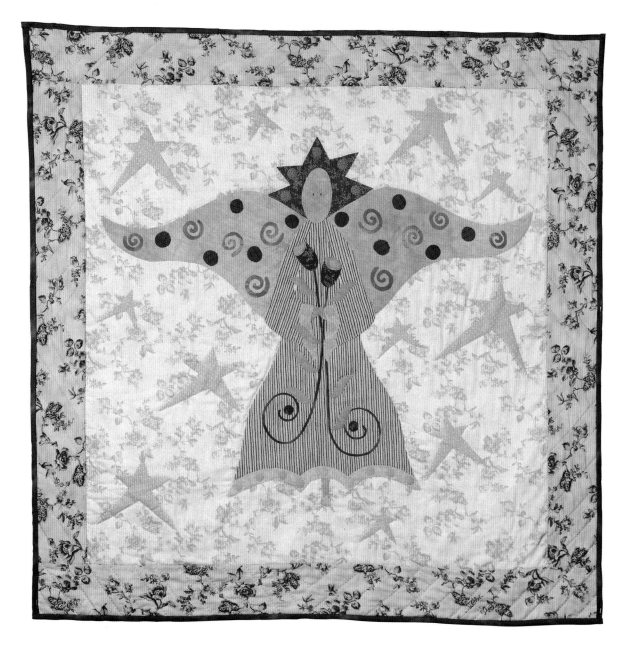

Finished Quilt Size: 44" x 44"

Fabric Requirements

- Appliqué block background –
  1⅛ yd. off-white floral print
- Quilt border – ⅝ yd. tan with pink floral print
- Angel dress & sleeves – fat quarter pastel stripe
- Angel wings – ¾ yd. tan
- Stars – fat quarter gold with white polka dots
- Backing – 2⅔ yds. dark pink floral print
- Binding – ½ yd. dark green

Scraps for Appliqué:
- Angel head, hands & feet – 6" sq. tan
- Trim on dress – 6" x 18" pale pink print

- Circles (trim & headband) –
  10" sq. pale yellow
- Halo – 10" sq. brown
- Circles on halo – 6" sq. blue-gray
- Flowers & circles on stems –
  6" sq. dark pink
- Inner flower – 4" sq. light pink
- Flower centers – 3" sq. yellow
- Stems – 6" x 18" dark green
- Leaves – 8" sq. pale green
- Circles on wings – 8" sq. dark gray
- Spirals on wings – 12" sq. medium blue

Cutting Instructions

Block Background:
Cut 36½" sq.

Quilt Border:
First cut: cut four 4½" strips 44" wide
Second cut: cut two of the strips 40½" long

Cut two of the strips 36½" long
Cut two squares 4½" x 4½"

Quilt Binding:
Cut five 2" x 44/45" strips

Giving Furniture a Vintage Look

Quilt Assembly Instructions

Milk paint is great for giving furniture a vintage look. Milk paint is a natural product that was used for centuries before we had the chemicals that we have now. You can buy milk paint in powder form, mix it with water, and use whatever thickness you want.

A friend of mine and I used to use milk paint on new furniture – sometimes furniture that her husband had just made. We would make kind of a thick paint mixture, paint it on, then blow the drying paint with a blow dryer to crack the paint. Then we'd go over it with an antiquing gel or a dark wax finish, rubbing it down so we stained the wood that was showing through.

Another trick we used was to rub a wax candle onto the furniture before it was painted. We'd rub the wax where the furniture would naturally get the most wear as it was used. For example, on a trunk, the lid would naturally be worn more right where it was held to be lifted, and the trunk corners would get worn from bumping things. So we would take a candle and rub it on the lid and corners. Then we'd paint the trunk, and dry the paint with a blow dryer, and the paint would not stick to the candle wax. After the paint was dry we'd lightly sand the worn areas to blend the dry paint with the wood. Finally, we'd go over it with a stain or wax stain. The exposed wood would be stained, but the waxed areas would also show through.

Block Assembly Instructions:
Appliqué the block. Make two small stitches for the angel's eyes, as pictured.

Quilt Assembly Instructions:
1. Sew a square to one end of each side border, as shown. Press flat.
2. Sew the top and bottom border to the quilt center block.
3. Add the side borders to complete the quilt top.

Suggested Hand or Machine Quilting:
Outline appliqué patches. Diagonal lines on border, meeting in a V at border center.

Two vertical stitches ⅝" apart make angel eyes.

INSTALLING THE
MAGIC BOOK™ SOFTWARE

1. Insert the disc into your computer's CD-ROM drive.
2. Click on Start.
3. Point to Settings.
4. Click on Control Panel.
5. Double-click the Add/Remove Programs icon.
6. Click on the Install button.
7. Follow the instructions on the screen.

MORE SOFTWARE AND BOOKS
FROM THE ELECTRIC QUILT COMPANY

The Electric Quilt Company develops computer software and books especially for quiltmakers. We invite you to find out how much fun your computer can be! EQ products make it easy for you to use your skills with color and pattern to design and create your own quilts, blocks and patterns.

ELECTRIC QUILT
Complete quilt design program

Includes over 10,000 quilt blocks and fabrics that are ready for you to design with so it's easy for the beginner. If you need more advanced tools, you can draw your own design, scan your own fabric, design your own quilt layout. Foundation piecing, appliqué, yardage calculation – EQ does it all!

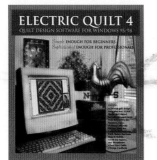

BLOCKBASE 2
The ultimate quilt block resource

Barbara Brackman's ***Encyclopedia of Pieced Quilt Patterns*** on CD. All new Windows 95/98 version. Over 3,500 quilt patterns. Every pieced block from 1835-1970! Includes all pieced blocks from ***Kansas City Star, Carrie Hall***, and hundreds of other collections!

SEW PRECISE
Foundation patterns galore

Select a block, print the foundation pattern, sew by number right on the paper pattern – it's "sew . . . precise!" Collections 1&2 come bundled together – over 1,100 patterns, new and traditional. Collection 3 has 600 patterns from designer Shirley Liby.

STASH
Fabric store on a CD

See the newest fabric lines or ones you've had in your own fabric stash. This software lets you color-coordinate fabrics for your projects. Use alone or with EQ quilt design software. Thousands of fabrics in each edition – published twice a year.

STAYING IN TOUCH WITH
THE ELECTRIC QUILT COMPANY

The Electric Quilt Company
419 Gould Street, Suite 2
Bowling Green, OH 43402 USA

Phone: 419-352-1134 (9am to 5pm EST)
Fax: 419-352-4332
To order: 800-356-4219

sales@electricquilt.com   www.electricquilt.com
Our products are available at a quilt store near you.